SEARCHING FOR A STAR

Zachary Breland

To anyone trapped in a seemingly hopeless situation, still searching for light…

Never Give Up.

contents

BECAUSE MY INSECURITY DEMANDS AN INTRODUCTION

If you're reading this, then from the bottom of my heart, thank you. Publishing has always been a dream; but to see it realized causes me to swell with both pride and terror, especially with a work so personal.

This short collection of poetry is fueled by an unrelenting battle with anxiety. I knew I wanted to make clear how exhausting it is battling your own mind, especially when you know what to do and what you need but nonetheless feel powerless. The lows are depressing, and the highs feel false, like at any moment it could all come crashing down.

My mother's go-to adage is what informed the structure of this collection; everything seems worse at night, but in the morning, the mind is a little clearer. However, even when you've finally found a little peace, darkness lurks just under the surface; and just the thought of being consumed is enough to drive you back into the cycle.

Despite appearances, I wanted to end on a hopeful note; I know there's light at the end of the tunnel, and I'm determined to keep walking until I get there.

Zachary Breland

I put pen to paper
and the blood from
every wound,
fresh and withered,
pours onto the page.
In return,
ink runs up and over
every cut and burn,
crafting scars,
and helping me heal.

the demons dance at dusk

future/forever

I'll always wonder
if my mother
glimpsed the future;
if the tears in her eyes
as she lifted me off the floor
were from knowing
I would always struggle
to pick myself up.

one track mind

My head swivels
in every direction,
back and forth with
the voices that crowd the air.

But it's all muffled;
white noise to the
one thought
that paralyzes my mind.

What did I do wrong?

drown out

I cover my ears
and scream,
trying to quiet the voice in my head.
But every time I do
it just gets louder

    and Louder

      and LOUDER

within the panel

If only life was a collection
of one-shot comic books;
thoughts just mere words,
detached from the mind
with no lasting impact.
Actions just instances,
retconned after the
turn of a few pages.

circling

Thoughts circle my head
like hawks hovering above prey;
ready to strike regardless
of how unprepared I am.

the right response?

Sometimes I don't respond,
not because I don't want to
(God Knows I do),
but because I'm afraid
that my reply
won't be enough
to keep you interested.

before I burn

Kindred souls are hard to find;
survivors of the fire
that can detect the gas
before I ignite.

insanity

Even with the pain,
even after the fall,
I continue to do
what hurts most of all.

19

It was the year that broke me,
redefined who I was,
casted my entire life
in a dark spotlight,
overwhelming and painful.

My mind,
unknowingly on the brink,
unraveled faster than I could keep up.

Some days I fear
I've grown no further
since then;
that I'm still that kid,
lost and alone,
scared of my own shadow.

blame it on the devil

Red whispers in my mind,
sinister words that sound sweet,
offering paths of pain
that I take regardless.

lifeline

I was hanging on for dear life
when you decided to let go.

Now I'm stranded.

will it ever let up?

Sometimes
the clouds break
and I feel the tiniest bit of warmth.

But it's deceiving.

Five minutes later
and it all comes crashing down.

grainy

Some days I
open my eyes,
vision hazy with grain,
and for the briefest
of moments
I have hope I
can change the channel
from this pain.

But the remote is out of reach.

distorted reflections

Every day the same perception,
yet I drag myself
to the mirror for judgement.

Ugly.

Fat.

Disgusting.

Unworthy.

unanswered

My knees are stained red from
the years I spent kneeling before Him,
pleading for Him to
take away all the pain.

But he stopped answering,
so, I no longer try,
and I fend for myself.

more than I can carry

The ground quivers
with every step,
my body sinking deeper and deeper
as each new though latches on;
it's invisible,
but it weighs me down every day,
and threatens to bury me alive.

lifeless

I've grown numb
to the wonders of every day;
living life comatose,
a marionette on Fate's cruel strings.

before I'm buried

I scrape away
at walls of dirt,
grime collecting
under my fingernails.

I dug this grave years ago,
and every time I think
I've clawed my way out,
something knocks me back in.

a faulty lamp

If I can't
drag myself
out of this cave,
how can I
expect to show
others the light?

2 a.m.

Curled against
the familiar fabric
of my couch,
lying motionless,
feeling for safety.

Please…
all I want
is to stop spinning
through this vicious
cycle of thought.

compromised

I once savored the safety of sleep,
the walled-off break in time and space
in which I could hide
from the thoughts that chase me.

But now they have invaded,
and there's nowhere left to cower,
to rest.

Zachary Breland

nightmares & dreams

*fun*house

Guttural laughter erupts
from their mouths.
Everywhere I turn,
fingers jab in my direction,
mocking bodies and jeering faces
cutting off escape.
I try to scream,
but I can't;
tightened thread through my lips
prevent them from parting.

I'm powerless to do anything but cower,
tears pooling at my feet.

I furiously rub my eyes,
trying to stop the bleeding,
when all sound dies.

I peer above my hands
but freeze when I see
that every face has been replaced with my own.

history

His weary palm
rests upon a leather clothed tome.
Ink pools from every wrinkled print,
every crevice,
every quirk,
every moment,
every scar.

With his final breath,
it seeps through each page,
branding like wildfire
his story.

balloon watching

She cut
what I thought was
my lifeline.
Instead, every doubt and fear
floated away.

But she left
because I couldn't stop
looking up,
waiting for it to pop
and come crashing down.

flickr

Head fixed on the ceiling,
futilely hoping for a chance.

The lights off,
waiting for a message
to bring color to my room.

Our favorite movie plays,
but it's only white noise
as I stare blankly.

As the night ticks by,
my already waning confidence
starts to fade completely.

tough love

Sometimes
it doesn't matter how much
you try to poke a hole;
there's no unraveling a quilt
that's already stood the test of time.

rocky waters

Broken hearts are like
paper boats lost at sea;
dissolving as they
drift aimlessly,
destined to crumple
under the smallest wave.

in this moment

The hazy sun,
half-dipped in the horizon,
glinting off the gold
trapped in his sweaty fingers.

With every millisecond that ticks by,
she watches his eyes resist
the nervous urge to avert his gaze.

Her hair whips across her face,
the salty ocean aroma intermingling
with lathered-in lavender.

converging

I stand alone
on the same platform every night,
an eerie silence filling the station.

It starts as a low rumble,
but it grows until the ground shakes,
pillars cracking,
dust falling from above.

A shill cry rings from
the announcement system.
I cover my ears,
but the bleeding doesn't slow.

Dark at first,
the arrival boards furiously flash,
ALL TRAINS ARRIVING NOW.

The platform starts to narrow,
but I'm rooted to the spot,
unable to run,
as they begin plowing by,
one after another without break.

mechanical fingers

Her face, flush and damp,
emerald eyes suffocated by puffy pink.
Her chest expanding and deflating rapidly,
sobs barely escaping her throat.

His cold, hollow hand,
placed on her shoulder,
his mechanical breaths
purposely timed with hers.

And still she cries.

laying to rest

She wades through
a field of roses and lilies,
carnations, tulips, and the like;
a sea of color
dwarfing her lifeless grey.

Tears rain from her dimming eyes,
landing on the vivid members
of the efflorescence
through which she drifts.

Petals vanish,
only to start sprouting
from under her skin,
flowers blossoming across
every inch of her body.

on the level of angels

I stumbled upon an angel,
unconscious,
lying in the grass.

I took not her wings,
for I learned from the folly
of my last attempt.

I took not her unblemished gown,
for I knew nothing could change
their scowls and stares.

Instead I reached
for the fading circle of light
floating inches above her head.

I thought maybe, just maybe,
I could momentarily break the cloud
constantly suffocating my mind.

grace

He turned toward the Earth,
for He heard the cries
of His angel.

He witnessed the act,
a girl driven by her desire
to stop the suffering.

He watched as the girl wrapped
her blood-soaked hands
around the fading halo.

Now, seared from the inside out,
by a flame no man could handle,
she lies withering away.

In His corporeal form,
He kneels in the grass,
holding her head in His lap.

"My child...
was it worth the cost?"

With the shadow of a smile
spread across her lips, she replies.

"I didn't know what else to try."

blinding

I remember the waterfall,
a cascade of droplets freckling her face,
the refraction of the sun
making visible the glow
that had defined her for so long.

shattered possibilities

Every night,
echoes of your infant cries
play tricks on my restless mind.

Every night,
I stare at the ceiling,
listening for the creak of the kitchen door.

Every night,
I let static illuminate the room,
waiting for you to choose another movie.

Every night,
I sweat in terror,
scared I can't be there for you.

Every night,
I'm on my knees,
pleading for God to give you back.

captive

Legs against my chest,
head squeezed between knees,
fingernails digging into skin.

I cower in the corner of my cell,
trying to shield myself
from the etchings
that dance along the walls,
a gallery of the worst moments of life,
on repeat,
imprinting on my mind forever.

devoid

Hands brushing against skin,
desperately searching for warmth.
Love.
Fingertips scratching the surface
of a soulful host,
a vessel of pure emotion.

... nothing.

A hollow carcass
where a heart should be.
Cracked,
leaking.
Broken,
empty.

Lost.

sculpting desire

Wading through red,
trembling, twitching.
Grasping for a tremor,
a beat.

Fingers curling around the surface,
tugging,
yanking,
severing.

In the palm of your hand,
the crimson fades.
Cold.
Pale.
Vulnerable.

A canvas.

left without

A symphony of screams,
trapped within a silent body,
the newly purged canvas.

A face with no features,
sunken caves where light once shone.

With every splash of red,
distortion where words once stumbled;
five fingers pushing against fabric,
desperate to be free.

shame

Faces, to which
I've only ever aspired
to model myself after,
look down in disgust,
at how far the apple
has fallen.

With every look of disdain,
I shrink

smaller

and

smaller,

tiny enough
for them to avoid.

when I dream of flying

My wings carve
through those misshapen
puffs of white
floating far above
the city.

The sun refracts
off my scales and
paints the clouds
a rainbow palette.

I barrel forward,
gliding through an intermittent
tunnel of technicolor.

it never lasts long

As night descends across the sky,
I climb ever higher,
basking in the glow
of a full moon.

A howling screech pierces my ears,
and from the clouds below,
figures of pure darkness ascend.

I sense their malice,
but I'm paralyzed to evade
as they latch onto my body.

Their claws dig at my scales,
ripping away my iridescence,
my vibrancy fading.

I cry as they tear off my wings,
crimson scattering through the air,
and I start to fall.

confessions

The little leaf, moon bathing
beside my torn-up shoes,
picking a spot as far from my dastardly shadow
as possible.

My hands feverishly feel around
for the nothing in my pockets.

I'm still waiting.
She hasn't said anything
and I'm still waiting.
I don't dare look.

I blink as my gaze
shifts towards the sky.
It's as if the moon sent
an invitation to the stars
to shine brighter with it.
But they won't.
Not yet,
if at all.

I level my head
and my eyelids spring open.
Under the moon,
her eyes sparkle,
and meet mine.

A group of wind streams rustle
an invitation to the residents
of the nearby cherry blossom.
The petals accept without hesitation,
following the wind in its path between her and I.
The moon-bathed leaf
ascends to join its friends,
a spot of green among a flying sea of pink.
Across this ocean I spot her auburn hair
dancing to the whistle of the wind.

The contrasting colors fade from view.
The wind stops whistling,
her hair stops dancing,
clouds mask the moon.
She glides her hand above her ear,
pushing back her hair.

"I love you too."

The clouds move to reveal
the moon shining brighter with
the help of a few friendly stars.

at the end/from the beginning

Entranced by the brilliant lights
scattered across
the endless canvas of space,
the stars she always
wished she could see.

Her mouth stretches with a grin
against the warmth
emanating from all around her.

He's not staring,
but she can feel the intensity
of His attention.

"Are you God?"
she playfully asks.

"To most."

Tone turning somber, she follows with
"Am I dead?"

"Is that what you desire?"

Once full of desperate conviction,
a comforting emptiness
now hollows her out;
clarity without confliction.

"I don't know."

The ground below illuminates,
a massive puzzle
that stretches forever;
each piece a moment in time.
With every step
as she drifts across,
memories ripple to life,
and all the feelings
she previously couldn't feel
came back to her.

And for the first time,
in a long time,
she cries.

the angels sing at sunrise

breaking through

Eyelids spring open
to the dust drifting through air,
illuminated by a strip of light
lying across my sheets.

In that moment,
I hear only the sounds
of feathered friends
celebrating the start of a new,
clear,
day.

anticipating the sound

Unaccustomed to the silence,
I move gingerly through the house,
the crack of my ankles
sinking into concrete walls.

I can't help but shake,
near paralyzed by the possibility
that my mind will find a way
to kill this newfound quiet.

kaleidoscope

It's like someone
finally stopped rotating
a kaleidoscope;
blurry images
are now clear,
the world no longer spins,
and everything is
falling into place.

second home

Well-worn paths,
imprints of my mistakes
pressed into each and every tile.

Farther along,
the gaping cracks I would fall through,
to let the darkness of
pervasive thought consume me.

Today I avoid them;
but how long before I
WANT
to jump back in?

call to inaction

As the day wears on,
my steps are labored,
my feet drag,
and my knees buckle.

I realize then that
the ground is calling.

always in motion

Breath ragged,
chest heaving,
the wind does nothing to
cool the sweat
pouring down my face.

Legs ache and wobble,
but I push and I run,
from the thought
I thought was gone.

pulling me back

There are times
when my mind
pulls me back in,
and I can do
nothing
but sit in the dark
with my demons,
hoping the moment passes.

daymares

All eyes
centered on me,
welling with tears.

Arms reach desperately,
but hands crumple
against an invisible wall.

Mouths move,
but no sound escapes.

With every passing second,
more of me disappears.

I know they care,
but I can't feel it.

rescue mission

Entire days,
devoted to searching
for the sputtering flame
deep inside,
the one that crackles,

"I matter."

swimming lessons

Stripped bare,
wading out to where
the seas threaten to consume
both heart and mind.

I once stood upon the shore,
terrified of being swallowed by the pain,
self-inflicted or otherwise.

But now I break the surface,
diving headfirst,
letting the blue surround me.

It's time I learned to breathe
under the pressure.

drunk on fairy tales

To keep the thoughts at bay,
I dive into uncharted,
yet familiar waters,
a sea of journeys
not my own;
tales of killer smiles
and weeping trees,
talking animals
and faraway plants,
all in the hope of escaping
the one story I sometimes
wish I wasn't living.

a little fractured

I'm starting to realize
it's okay to not be okay,
to scream and to cry,
to let the feelings burst
through a mask
you can no longer keep whole.

faith

I hope one day
someone is willing to take a chance
on this broken path;
to trust that the destination
with be worth the journey.

compassion

Never belittle the struggle
of another person;
what you see as an afterthought,
may send someone else spiraling.

daydreams

Splintered in every direction,
a million shards of glass,
stained with my life;
moments of joy,
humility,
pain,
and love.

Each piece radiates
unexpected warmth,
even the darkest memories,
which sparkle with a beauty
I never thought hiding.

crumpled petals

People rarely notice
the beauty
they trample under foot.

They care not
for the subtle flowers
that don't catch their attention.

Just because they struggle
to shine brilliantly,
does not mean they hold no value.

okay with what stares back

This morning,
I passed by the mirror
without second thought.

I backpedaled just to check

And I was okay
with who I saw.

hopefall

A cacophony of colors,
flung from among the stars,
searching for those without hope,
streaking their way across the hopeful night,
teeming with a flutter,
a breath,
a beat.

EUPHORIA

A giddiness in my bones,
legs itching to
propel my body forward.
Though surrounded by darkness,
warmth spreads through my limbs,
light emanating from
somewhere deep inside.
Faint at first,
but it grows to a blinding pitch,
cutting at the seemingly eternal despair,
revealing something unexpectedly beautiful.

Acknowledgements

A work like this (and a person like me) isn't pushed to publication without the support and tough love of friends and family willing to push me out of my comfort zone.

Sam, we can go from singing ABBA to discussing the psychological reasoning behind substance abuse, all within the span of ten minutes. You understand me, you relate to me, and you challenge me. In the months leading to this, you encouraged me to put myself out there, even though I was unsure if my words could find a platform. You've been my promoter when I'm too scared to share my voice. Without you, I would never have crossed the finish line.

Natasha, you are the big sister I never knew I wanted. In the short time we've known each other, you've become family. You hear me out, tell me like it is, and call me on my bull. A year and a half ago, you read just one poem and suggested I write a book. And since then, you 've continually pushed. Without you, this collection might not exist.

Annie, from short stories to poetry to ongoing family sagas (The Montgomery Boys), we have dealt in fiction for what feels like more than three years. A writing partner like no other, you helped rekindle my love for literature. Since day one, you have challenged me creatively, supporting my literary voice, no matter the form. The talent you possess is undeniable, and I can't wait for the day when you decide to share your imagination with the world.

And last but not least; Mom… without you, I would be in a much darker place than I am now. Thank you for your guidance and your love.

And to everybody who reads this, once again, with every aspect of my being, thank you.

THE AUTHOR

Sketch Courtesy of Sam